KU-241-206

A SLOTH'S GUIDE

TO TAKING IT EASY

Sarah Jackson

DOG 'N' BONE

Published in 2018 by Dog 'n' Bone Books
An imprint of Ryland Peters & Small Ltd
20-21 Jockey's Fields   341 E 116th St
London WC1R 4BW   New York, NY 10029

www.rylandpeters.com

10 9 8 7 6 5 4

A CIP catalog record for this book is available from
the Library of Congress and the British Library.

ISBN: 978 1 911026 57 0

Printed in Slovenia

Illustrator: Sarah Jackson
Designer: Eliana Holder

CONTENTS

INTRODUCTION

Living in the 21st century can be pretty exciting, but with everything moving so fast it can also be rather tiring. It's now so easy to feel the pressures of modern life.

We think it's time that everybody slowed down, relaxed, and took more time to enjoy the little pleasures the simple life can bring. It's time we learned how to take things easy, but we also know that's easier said than done. That's why we've enlisted the help of an expert to help you along the way.

So put down that fast food, get rid of your super-speed broadband, and meet your mentor...

Brian.

Brian is a three-toed sloth.

I'M A
THREE-TOED
SLOTH!

6

As one of the world's most ancient and slowest creatures, the sloth has been around pretty much since the dawn of time.* This makes Brian the perfect mentor on your journey to taking a step back and slowing life down.

Don't just take our word for it—we'll let Brian talk you through what makes him the sloth for this job...

* We may have exaggerated that a little bit, but sloths are still pretty old.

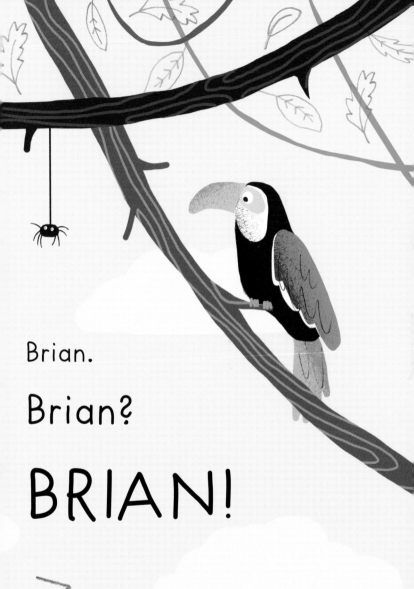

Brian.

Brian?

BRIAN!

Z

BRIAN THE SLOTH
Resume

EDUCATION: None

EMPLOYMENT
HISTORY: None

HOBBIES & INTERESTS:
Eating, sleeping, napping, hanging out with friends, socializing.

STRENGTHS:
Patience, a sunny disposition, relaxed and calm under pressure, can communicate with creatures from all walks of life.

WEAKNESSES: Running, time management.

PERSONAL STATEMENT:
I'm a calm and dependable sloth who has spent decades perfecting the art of relaxation. My optimistic outlook, combined with my laid-back attitude, makes me the ideal candidate for the role of relaxation guru.

So, with Brian's guidance we are going to look at some techniques and philosophies that will help slow down your pace of life and allow you to restore some inner calm.

I LIKE TO CALL THIS "TAKING IT EASY."

TAKING IT EASY (a definition):

The path of least resistance. Reduce
stress by suppressing the urge to rush,
push, or force yourself. Instead, learn
to accomplish your goals through
a relaxed and gentle approach to life.

Great. So now you know what to expect,
it's time to get started...

PART 1
BRIAN'S
TOP TIPS
ON HOW TO
TAKE IT EASY

By following these tried-and-tested methods,
you'll end up so relaxed you will be
horizontal. That's a handy position to
be in—it's perfect for sleeping. Trust me,
I'm a sloth.

Now let us begin...

TIP 1: EAT HEALTHILY

Eating plenty of fresh food will help keep you fit and healthy, and therefore ready to face whatever comes your way with ease! I like to make sure I get a balance of all the major food groups:

GREENS

FIBER

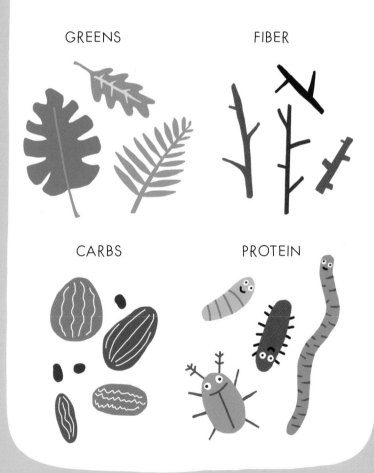

CARBS

PROTEIN

TIP 2: USE POSITIVITY MANTRAS

Feeling good starts with you. Take some time every day to tell yourself three things you like about yourself. These are your positivity mantras.

Stand in front of a mirror and repeat each mantra ten times.*

* If you can't count to ten, don't worry. Simply repeat the mantra over and over until you get bored.

If you're struggling to think up some positive mantras, maybe ask your friends to point out a few of your best features.

YOU'RE REALLY GOOD AT MUSICAL STATUES, BRIAN.

I LIKE YOUR HAIRY TOES.

YOU SMELL LIKE MY FAVORITE TREE GRUB.

TIP 3: SPEND TIME WITH LIKE-MINDED PEOPLE

Surrounding yourself with others who are on your wavelength will make you feel good about yourself. You'll find that time flies when you are together. Look for people with similar interests who you share things in common with—you'll find that conversation flows more naturally.

A good dose of daily stretchi[ng] reduce any muscle tension th[at] throughout the day, but will [also] your energy levels.

I've heard lots of people talk called yoga. It sounds interest easy enough to practice stret[ch] those hard-to-reach leaves an[d]

Meeting new people can be fun, but sometimes making small talk can be hard work. To make things easier for yourself, try using these suggestions for easy conversation starters:

TIP 4: STRETCH REGULA[R]

Stretching has so many p[...]
It's a great form of exer[cise]
require too much effort.

TIP 5: REMOVE NEGATIVITY AND THINGS THAT WEIGH YOU DOWN

As we pass through life, we can become bogged down with stresses and responsibilities—both mentally and physically. These pressures can make you feel heavy and burdened—those kinds of negative vibes aren't good for you.

Once in a while, take some time to let go of whatever it is that's weighing you down... Just take a deep breath, release the load, and you'll feel so much better for it.

TIP 6: MAKE TIME TO ENJOY YOUR FAVORITE THINGS

When you have a demanding lifestyle, it's easy to get caught up in the day-to-day slog of chores and "things you NEED to do." That's no fun!

It's important to make time for the activities you enjoy doing. Some people have hobbies, such as gardening, baking cakes, or playing sports. My favorite pastime is sleeping, and when I'm asleep I dream of all the fun things I've got up to that day.

Mid-morning nap

Eating a leaf

HI BRIAN!

Chats with Phil the Snail

Afternoon nap

Eating another leaf

TIP 7: TRY PHYSICAL CONTACT

That's right, a good old-fashioned cuddle is a great mood lifter! It helps to hug another living object for the ultimate authentic experience—luckily I've always got plenty of willing pals to choose from here in the rainforest. However, a pillow or pile of leaves will do if you don't have any friends nearby.

Research has shown that stroking a pet can be calming and even help lower blood pressure. I don't have a pet, but it doesn't matter—there are so many animals in the rainforest who don't mind me giving them a stroke when I feel like it.

CAREFUL BRIAN!

TIP 8: USE THE POWER OF PLANTS

Harness the energy of mother nature and indulge in some natural remedies. Herbal teas have been used for thousands of years to aid relaxation, to promote a sense of calm, and even to help you get a good night's sleep (I don't need any help with that, but it can't hurt). You can buy them readymade or if you're feeling adventurous, why not go foraging for some free organic ingredients!

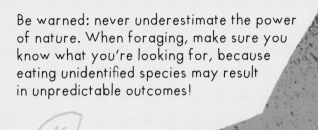

Be warned: never underestimate the power of nature. When foraging, make sure you know what you're looking for, because eating unidentified species may result in unpredictable outcomes!

TIP 9: DON'T COMPARE YOURSELF TO OTHERS

It's hard not feel envious at other people's achievement sometimes, but it's important to remember that their successes are not your failures. Try not to be jealous of others, because this will only make you feel bad.

BRIAN, DID YOU KNOW I CAN RUN AT OVER 100 MPH?! AND I CAN JUMP REALLY HIGH. I'M PRETTY GOOD AT EVERYTHING.

Plus, to be the best at everything requires persistence and hard work. No thanks! Try this instead: whenever someone does something good, congratulate them and then, when they're not listening, quietly remind yourself of something positive you've done.

GOOD FOR YOU PAUL.
(*WHISPER*: I DID A POOP
THE SIZE OF AN ARMADILLO
LAST WEEK.)

TIP 10: TAKE A DEEP BREATH

Let's face it, some people just can be really, really annoying.

Don't let anger get the better of you. Instead, take a deep breath, close your eyes, think of a relaxing place, and slowly count to ten.*

* WARNING: Sometimes this technique may result in you falling asleep. That's OK—just go with it.

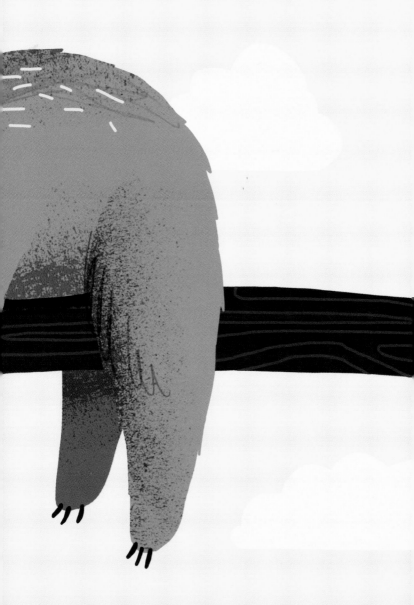

SORRY, I needed a short nap break...
Anyway...

TIP 11: GET BACK TO BASICS

Sometimes it's good to appreciate the simple things in life and leave the shackles of the modern world behind. And what better way to do so than surround yourself with the beauty of nature?!

Once a week, I like to leave the confines of my tree and the pressures of the modern world to go for a swim. No phones, no emails, no beeps, alarms, or noise—it's just me, the water, and my own thoughts.

UM... THAT'S NOT STRICTLY TRUE, BRIAN.

YEAH, WE CAN SEE YOU.

HIDE YOUR EYES, SON.

TIP 12: EMBRACE MODERN TECHNOLOGY

I know, I know... I just told you to get back to basics. HOWEVER, sometimes modern technology can be your best friend, making life easier and allowing you to experience the world at your finger tips (or toes).

GNA B L8

Learning text lingo has helped me save hours of precious time that would have otherwise been spent on writing full sentences. It is now spent on doing things I enjoy—like sleeping.

It can be hard work traveling from tree to tree, so sometimes I like to talk to my friends on the telephone. It's much easier.

HI DARREN!
IT'S BEEN AGES!
WHERE HAVE
YOU BEEN?

I'M RIGHT HERE,
BRIAN.

TIP 13: TRY ONLINE DATING

It's great when you meet someone you're attracted to in real-life situations—like on the way to the watering hole or when rummaging through a termite mound. Sadly these encounters are often few and far between, which can make finding a meaningful relationship feel like hard work. That's where online dating comes in handy!

There are hundreds of potential partners at the swipe of my claw—sometimes I can swipe through as many as 10 in a day!

And I've met some very exotic characters from all walks of life!

TIP 14: LIGHTEN UP AND HAVE A LAUGH

Why take life so seriously? If you're permanently carrying a frown around, then it's time to start thinking positively and have some fun. I like to make myself, and others, laugh at least twice a day—try learning some jokes and practice them on your friends.

WHY WAS THE OWL SO SAD?

HE WAS OWL BY HIMSELF, BECAUSE HE HAD NO FRIENDS!

Remember, not everyone likes jokes and some folks just don't have a great sense of humor. Look to find a captive audience who like to have a laugh and you'll find that your jokes go a long long way.

I'VE NOT EVEN GOT TO THE PUNCH LINE YET GUYS!

TIP 15: RELAX WITH A GOOD BOOK

A great way to unwind is to sit down with a good book. Some people like romances or thrillers or detective novels, but I prefer something a little lighter—like a magazine (it's much easier to nap between stories!). Plus, I love getting an insight into the lives of others—it's so juicy!

WATCH THE BUGS COME SWARMING

EAU
DE
POOP

TRUE STORIES

THAT'S JUNGLE LIFE!

TALES OF A DESPERATE HOUSE SPIDER

I ATE MY OWN HUSBAND

TIP 16: TAKE A VACATION

Sometimes it's great to just get away from it all—a change of scenery can work wonders for the soul.

Just remember, a trip away doesn't have to be a far-flung adventure—as long as your time off gives you a break from your day-to-day life, you'll benefit from the relaxation it can bring.

HAVING A GOOD TIME, BRIAN?

BRIAN'S TREE

I'M ON VACATION. BACK SOON (MAYBE).

I like to go to a place where I can really put my feet up and be waited on hand and foot.

TREE GRUB, SIR?

49

TIP 17: LOOK AT THINGS FROM A NEW PERSPECTIVE

Sometimes it's easy to get into a negative mindset and focus on all the bad things around you. This is not helpful to anyone! You need to shift your way of thinking, focusing on the good things that life has to offer instead of the negatives.

Whenever I feel down, I like to find my favorite rose-tinted glasses and all of a sudden life doesn't seem so bad at all!

HELLO
BEAUTIFUL
WORLD!
YOU'RE
LOOKING
ROSY!

TIP 18: BREAK THINGS DOWN

We all lead such busy lives, and when you have lots to do it's easy to forget things that might be important. I find writing a to-do list helps me keep my brain in order and it means I can tackle things one job at a time.

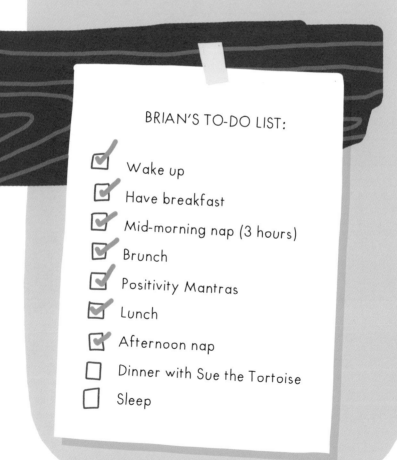

BRIAN'S TO-DO LIST:

- ☑ Wake up
- ☑ Have breakfast
- ☑ Mid-morning nap (3 hours)
- ☑ Brunch
- ☑ Positivity Mantras
- ☑ Lunch
- ☑ Afternoon nap
- ☐ Dinner with Sue the Tortoise
- ☐ Sleep

Sometimes noting everything down can seem a little daunting once you realize just how much you have to do. Try to tackle one thing at a time, that way it will seem more easily achievable.

BUT I'VE GOT A LIST AS LONG AS MY ARM BRIAN.

GET SHORTER ARMS THEN JEFF!

TIP 19: IGNORANCE IS BLISS

When things really get too much, sometimes it's just best not to think about it. Why stress yourself out by worrying about everything, when you can just forget about it all and chill out instead?

One of my online friends told me this is called "burying your head in the sand."

We don't have sand around here so you just have to be inventive...

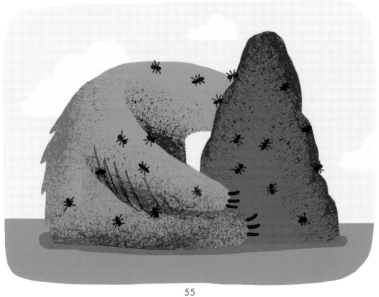

TIP 20: MY BEST ADVICE YET

We've come to my final tip for taking it easy. I hope that you've found them useful and are well on your way to feeling nice and relaxed.

If these tips haven't worked, then this final piece of advice should do the trick...

JUST CHILL OUT, YEAH?

THAT'S RIGHT—LIGHTEN UP AND CHILL OUT.

STOP MOANING, STOP STRESSING, STOP RUSHING, AND STOP WORRYING. JUST CALM DOWN AND CHILL OUT—IT REALLY IS THAT EASY! ISN'T THAT RIGHT, GUYS?

PART 2
ANCIENT WISDOM

When it comes to relaxing and taking things easy, I'm not the only guru.

I'd like to leave you with some ancient wisdom from some of my favorite philosophers that you may find useful.

"SLEEP IS THE BEST MEDICATION."

Dalai Lama

"IT DOESN'T MATTER
HOW SLOWLY YOU GO,
SO LONG AS YOU
DO NOT STOP."

Confucius

"BABY DON'T WORRY... ABOUT A THING.
'COS EVERY LITTLE THING...
IS GONNA BE ALRIGHT."

Bob Marley

ACKNOWLEDGMENTS

I'd like to dedicate this book to my husband Nick and our cat George, who provide me with daily inspiration on how to be more sloth-like and seek out the easy life.